FINDING

YOUR

SONG

FINDING

YOUR

SONG

DAN McCOLLAM

Published by
iWAR (INSTITUTE of WORSHIP ARTS RESOURCES) and
SOUNDS OF THE NATIONS
6391 Leisure Town Road, Vacaville, California 95687

Songs by Brian and Jenn Johnson, used by permission of Brian and Jenn Johnson Ministries, Bethel Music.

ISBN 978-0-9851863-1-9

Printed in the United States of America

First Edition: June 2012

Table of Contents

Introduction

❧

Sing to the LORD a new song; sing to the LORD, all the earth (Psalm 96:1).

Everyone can and should write a praise and worship song. Once upon a time I thought that worship writing was only for the stunningly talented, well-connected musicians and professionals in musical cities like Nashville, Los Angeles, and New York. Or perhaps only the giant churches with television shows were the ones to write songs that influence cultures. This wrong thinking stifled my own passion for writing songs to the Lord for many years. I mean, what's the point of writing a song if it is never going to go anywhere?

Then I met a young peasant girl in China. Though she was a junior high dropout who couldn't read or write music, she composed one thousand beautiful praise and worship songs. This young lady didn't play a musical instrument, wasn't on staff at a big church, she didn't have a record deal, yet her songs (called the "Canaan Hymns") are the main worship anthems of hundreds of millions of believers in China.

Down through the years, I learned that many of my favorite worship songs were written by ordinary people, not superstars or musical masters. The worship classic "I Love You Lord" was written by a housewife living in a trailer on the high desert of Oregon. "Lord, I Lift Your Name on High," another worship classic, was composed by a part-time worship leader working full-time in the computer business. These songs—written by ordinary people—have blessed and empowered millions of believers around the world to worship God in spirit and in truth.

More than that, I was reminded that the song that is sung one time in the prayer closet before the Lord is often the most treasured song of all. Ultimately, the value of a song is determined by its power in the secret place, not the market place.

Currently, I travel around the world encouraging and training worship writers, singers, and musicians to write and record their own praise and worship songs in their unique styles and languages. I believe everyone has a song locked inside. Psalm 40:2-3 says:

> *He lifted me up out of a slimy pit, out of the mud and mire; he set my feet on a rock and gave me a firm place to stand. He put a new song in my mouth, a hymn of praise to our God.*

The intent of this book is to help unlock the song that is inside of you. The lessons are simple presentations with examples that help us recognize seven sources for inspiration. I've drawn from the wisdom of the most passionate and popular worship writers of our day.

In this book, I've partnered with songwriters and worship leaders Brian and Jenn Johnson from Bethel Church in Redding, California, for song examples. Their songs are currently sweeping the globe as a musical representation of a transformational movement.

Whether you are just beginning your journey as a worship writer or are an experienced writer looking for a fresh idea, it is my prayer that interaction with *Finding Your Song* will help give you the tools to craft a new song of praise in your heart to the Lord.

Chapter One

Scripture Songs

The Scripture is without question the best source for beginner or advanced songwriters.

Let the word of Christ dwell in you richly as you teach and admonish one another with all wisdom, and as you sing psalms, hymns and spiritual songs with gratitude in your hearts to God (Colossians 3:16).

Notice the obvious connection between songs and the Word of Christ. In our songwriting workshops, I always encourage new composers to start writing from the Scripture. The Word of God possesses several characteristics that make it the strongest source of inspiration for worship writers.

First of all, the infallible quality of Scripture allows the songwriter to focus on issues of melody and structure over content and lyric. Put simply: songs from Scripture can be easier to write because so much of the lyric is already provided. Many beginning writers struggle most in the area of lyrics. By using ideas or phrases from Scripture as your primary lyric, you already have a time-tested, God-approved lyric for your worship song. That's a great starting place.

Another helpful thing about Scripture songs is that the Bible provides a wide array of solid theological themes and phrases that are instantly accessible for the worship writer. What to write about, or choosing a song subject, can be another potential roadblock for songwriters and worship writers. The Bible speaks to every area of life and answers some of the heart's deepest questions. The fact that Scripture is "God-breathed"[1] allows the writer the unique opportunity to partner with the Holy Spirit in the songwriting process and to speak on important subjects from heaven's perspective.

Scripture songs also possess universal song themes that appeal to virtually all worshipers regardless of their denomination, nationality, or culture. The most popular worship songs are not limited to geographical or denominational boundaries. This is the case for a well-crafted Scripture song; it's based on the world's most popular book. How can you not write a great worship song from such an amazing source?

Matt Redman is one of the most popular worship writers on the planet. His songs have impacted an entire generation of worshipers around the world. In an online interview, Matt made this statement in reference to Scripture songs:

> *"The good thing about the Bible is you can plagiarize it, and instead of getting sued you actually get encouraged."*[2]

Matt said of his own songwriting:

"I think more than anything, my songs are starting from Bible verses these days."[3]

So, Where Do You Begin?

By now I'm sure you are convinced that writing a worship song from Scripture is a great idea. Where do you begin? Great songs come from great ideas. These great song ideas should be crafted into the main point of the song called the "song hook." A song hook gets its name because like a fish hook, the song hook is the part of the song that catches your attention, sustains it, and pulls you along to a specific destination. The song hook is often the title of the song and is usually repeated lyrically or musically in the chorus section of the song.

To find the great idea in Scripture that will become your song hook, I encourage writers to start with an exercise I call "psalming." You can use any portion of Scripture for this exercise, but it is often easiest to begin in the book of Psalms. To get started, open your Bible to the book of Psalms and start singing the Word. Ignore forms, song structure, and the desire to match phrases. At this point you are not trying to write the song; just sing the verses and enjoy yourself "making music in your heart to the Lord."[4]

As you sing, you may notice particular lines or phrases that hold your attention. If one phrase seems thematically or melodically appealing, try repeating it several times. If no phrases stand out, keep on singing or try another Psalm or Bible version as your source.

Whenever a phrase grabs your attention you should record the idea on a small digital recording device, or, if you can score music, write it out so you won't forget the idea. Short phrases that are pleasing when repeated may form the foundation for a hook or chorus section.

Psalming is a great way to find these core hook ideas and have a meaningful worship experience at the same time.

After you've found your hook or chorus idea, you have a decision to make. What type of Scripture song will you create?

There are two basic types of Scripture songs: the literal and the inspired. Let's address the literal form first.

Literal Scripture Songs

When composing a literal Scripture song, all of the lyrics are lifted directly from the Scripture with little or no paraphrase. The verses for a literal Scripture song will most often be found in the neighboring verses where you first located your hook line or chorus.

It is permissible to drop a line or two of the Scripture passage from your song so long as eliminating these phrases does not alter the original meaning or proper interpretation of the passage. In the literal form, it is also acceptable to combine other literal Scripture verses from different book or chapter locations as long as the integrity of the meaning is maintained.

Inspired Scripture Songs

When choosing the inspired form of Scripture song, you may draw verse information from various Scriptures or add your own ideas. Inspired Scripture songs are based on Bible themes or adapted verses but don't literally follow the verse line-by-line.

Tommy Walker, a worship writer who has had over forty titles on the CCLI Top Ten song list, says that approximately half of his worship songs are taken directly from Scripture. Tommy recommends studying different Bible translations, paraphrases and commentaries related to your selected verse.

> *"This process frequently gives me new ideas so it's worth doing the work. Once I'm confident that I fully comprehend the text, I feel total freedom to be creative with it."[5]*

Inspired Scripture songs take their main theme or thought directly from Scripture but may also incorporate original ideas that support the theme.

Four Potential Snares in Scripture Songwriting

Brian Doerksen, another amazing worship writer and anointed teacher, warns us of two extremes that could render Scripture songs ineffective.

1. If you use the Scripture exactly as it is, watch out for a wooden, inflexible lyric that states truth but doesn't sing it.[6]

2. Be sure not to paraphrase inaccurately and end up saying something that Scripture never intended.

I would add these addition warnings when composing Scripture songs.

1. Avoid the tendency to become preachy and create a song that sounds more like a sermon than praise and worship.

2. Watch out for those moments when you are so inspired from the many truths of the Bible that you try to put too many thoughts into a single song. Different thoughts should be saved and used in their own songs since one of the goals of songwriting is to communicate a single theme in a unique and concise way.

Once you have chosen a song hook, you can begin writing the sections of your song. Two of the easiest and best tools for composing song sections are repetition and the list technique. Jenn and Brian Johnson have a great example of a Scripture song from their popular praise song, "O Taste and See" that uses both of these popular lyric composition tools.

O Taste and See

By Jenn and Brian Johnson

O Taste and see that the Lord is good
O Taste and see that the Lord is good to me
O Taste and see that the Lord is good
O Taste and see that the Lord is good to me

You have turned my mourning into dancing
Put off my rags and clothed me with gladness
And I will arise and I will praise you
I'll sing and not be silent

Chorus

O Lord my God
I will give thanks to you forever

Bridge

I will live only for you
I will lift these hands up to you
I will dance before you

I will shout it, I will shout it to you

This song combines two Scripture passages with some original ideas.

Psalm 34:8:

> *Taste and see that the LORD is good...*

Psalm 30:11-12:

> *You turned my wailing into dancing; you removed my sackcloth and clothed me with joy, that my heart may sing praise to you and not be silent. O LORD my God, I will give you thanks forever.*

As you can see, the first part of the verse is lifted literally from Scripture.

The line, "taste and see that the Lord is good" is repeated four times with the slight modification of the words "to me" appearing in line two and four. When you find a well-stated line or great song hook, don't be afraid to just repeat it. Repetition makes your song memorable, singable, and simple, which are all desirable qualities. Repetition can be used in any song section including chorus, verse, pre-chorus or bridge.

The second half of the verse is a pre-chorus song section that has some slight lyrical adaptations to make it more singable. A pre-chorus musically and lyrically sets up the chorus section. Notice that the inspiration for this lyric comes from a separate passage from the song hook but does not violate either Scripture's original intent.

This pre-chorus, beginning with the words, "You have turned...," is an example of what I call the "Double List" building technique. Notice how the pre-chorus is a simple list of three things God will do followed by a second list of three things the singer will do.

You have...

- Turned my mourning into dancing
- Put off my rags
- Clothed me with gladness

I will...

- Arise
- Praise you
- Sing and not be silent

You can find another example of the Double List building technique on the chorus of the worship classic, "Here I Am to Worship" by worship songwriter Tim Hughes.

The bridge section of Brian and Jenn's song is composed of original lines that are a response to the scriptural portions.

The bridge song section is crafted using another list building technique. This type of list is called a "Keyword List" because each line begins with the same word or phrase. "I will..." The list is completed with four declarations of intent.

I will...

- Live only for you
- Lift these hands up to you

- Dance before you
- Shout it to you

So in one song, Jenn and Brian model the literal, a proper adaptation of literal, and the inspired form of Scripture song as well as the two most popular techniques for crafting song sections: repetition and list building.

Now it's your turn. Complete the following exercises to deepen your understanding of writing a worship song from a scriptural source.

Practice Exercises

1) Practice the list building technique by extracting literal or inspired lists from Psalm 67 (below) to create song sections. Look for a main idea and melody that you can craft into a song hook. Consider using repetition of the song hook to compose a chorus section.

Psalm 67

May God be gracious to us and bless us and make his face to shine upon us, that your ways may be known on earth, your salvation among all nations.

May the peoples praise you, O God; may all the peoples praise you.

May the nations be glad and sing for joy, for you rule the peoples justly and guide the nations of the earth. Selah.

May the peoples praise you, O God; may all the peoples praise you. Then the land will yield its harvest, and God, our God, will bless us. God will bless us, and all the ends of the earth will fear him.

2) Make a regular habit of using the psalming exercise, i.e., singing the Scripture until you find interesting song hooks. Write down or record those great song hook ideas for development into Scripture songs. Consider using repetition and list building techniques to construct your song sections. Look for existing lists in Scripture passages that might be adapted to a modern song section.

3) Practice composing a Scripture song from each of the following song sources:

- Your favorite passage of Scripture
- A teaching portion of Scripture
- An unfamiliar passage

4) Below are some titles of inspired and literal Scripture songs that made the top CCLI charts of popular songs sung in American churches down through the years. You can find sound and lyric samples for most of these songs by searching the title and author on the internet. For each title that you are familiar with, determine whether the song would be classified as inspired or literal.

- "Let My Words Be Few" — by Matt and Beth Redman, Thankyou Music (Compare Eccl. 5:2)
- "Better is One Day" — by Matt Redman, Thankyou Music (Compare Ps. 84:10)
- "Open the Eyes of My Heart" — by Paul Baloche, Integrity's Hosanna! Music (Compare Eph. 1:18)
- "We Fall Down" — by Chris Tomlin, worshiptogether. com songs (Compare Rev. 4:10)
- "Blessed Be Your Name" — by Matt and Beth Redman, Thankyou Music (Compare Job 1:21)
- "As the Deer" — by Martin Nystrom, Maranatha Praise, Inc. (Compare Ps. 42)
- "Spirit of the Sovereign Lord" — by Andy Park, Mercy/Vineyard Publishing, Vineyard Songs Canada (Compare Ps. 61:2)
- "Remember Mercy" — by Brian Doerksen, Mercy/Vineyard Publishing, Vineyard Songs Canada (Compare Hab. 3:2)

What modern or classic Scripture songs would you add to this list? How would you classify these songs in terms of literal, paraphrased, or inspired?

Chapter Two

Great Themes

A second source of inspiration for worship writing is composing lyrics surrounding the great themes of Christianity. One key to breakthrough in worship is found in understanding that we worship at the level of our revelation. Increasing our revelation of who God is can deepen our worship experience. Exploring the great themes of Christianity can provoke in us a true spirit of praise and worship. Some of the major themes of our faith would include:

- God as our Father
- Deity of Christ
- Trinity
- Holy Spirit
- Salvation
- The Blood
- Resurrection
- Sanctification/Holiness
- Character and Nature of God
- Love of God

Consider the great theme of Rick Found's famous praise song, "Lord, I Lift Your Name on High."[7] In a mere nine lines, Rick lays out the entire death, burial, and resurrection of Christ in a simple, melodic way that makes you want to lift up His name. Sometimes we make the mistake of thinking that a great theme has to be loaded with heavy theology or a King James lyric. Rick's song demonstrates that inspiration from a great theme of the church can be communicated with simplicity and beauty.

A helpful resource for exploring great themes is old hymnals. Matt Redman says:

> "...reading old hymns can really open your eyes to new and fresh ways of looking at things."[8]

Matt's song "Take this World but Give Me Jesus" was inspired by a hymn from Fanny Crosby, a blind woman who composed more than eight thousand hymns and songs.

During the Protestant Reformation of the 16th century, songs like "A Mighty Fortress is Our God"[9] were loaded with singable theology to educate an illiterate population. Singing the church's great themes acquainted the common man with the deeper truths of the Word of God. The hymnals of that day became the theological textbooks of the church.

Our modern church has often been accused of lacking depth and substance in our songs. Perhaps it is time to sing again the great themes we believe to be true.

Great themes of the church can also be identified from outside reading sources. I have found personally that just reading through the table of contents of a theological book can inspire themes for a worship song. Books like A. W. Tozer's *Knowledge of the Holy*[10] can load your spirit with revelations of our Father that will inspire genuine praise and worship. Topical Bibles and devotionals are another helpful source for exploring great themes.

Brian Doerksen encourages worship writers to partner with pastors and teachers to write songs that reflect the themes of their local churches.

> *"Whenever you listen to teaching...ask the Lord, 'Should we be singing this?' Singing truth will greatly help our ability to remember important teaching."*[11]

Remember that praise and worship songs incorporating great themes don't have to be wordy and complicated. Great theme songs can be as simple as Brian Johnson's "Worthy is the Lamb That Was Slain."

Worthy Is the Lamb That Was Slain

By Brian Johnson

Worthy is the Lamb that was slain
Worthy is the Lamb that was slain
Worthy is the Lamb that was slain for me
For me, for me.

He gave it all for me

Worthy is the Lamb that was slain
Worthy is the Lamb that was slain
Worthy is the Lamb that was slain
For me, for me
He gave it all for me

Hallelujah, King forever
Hallelujah, give praise to our God
Hallelujah, King and Savior
We will sing

What makes this song so powerful is the importance of the subject matter combined with a majestic melody. Many of the songs sung around the throne of God chronicled in the book of Revelation are simple repetitive songs focused on the greatness, beauty and majesty of God. Songs that describe God's character, nature and attributes will always be at the core of true worship.

Consider popular worship classics like "How Great is Our God" by Chris Tomlin and friends. "Everlasting God" by Brenton Brown and Ken Riley, and "Holy is the Lord" by Chris Tomlin and Louie Giglio as other great examples. The power of these kinds of songs resides in the fact that they take us beyond superficial praise-babble into exploring themes that provoke and inspire us to focus on the greatness of God.

To further understand the importance of great themes, let's look at a passage in the fourth chapter of Revelation.

Each of the four living creatures had six wings and was covered with eyes all around, even under his wings.

> *Day and night they never stop saying: "Holy, holy, holy is the Lord God Almighty, who was, and is, and is to come"* (v. 8).

Notice that the four living creatures surrounding God's throne have some fascinating characteristics. First of all, they are covered with eyes all around, even under their wings. Strange creatures covered with eyeballs don't seem like they are chosen for their beauty. I believe that the reason these creatures are covered with eyes is so that they can have unlimited perspective of the One who sits on the throne. With these eyes they are constantly beholding new and greater things about who God is.

> *Great is the LORD and most worthy of praise; his greatness no one can fathom* (Psalm 145:3).

This is the key to how these creatures never tire praising God day or night. With their many eyes they are constantly beholding a greatness that no one can fathom. Each time they behold something new—or to a greater measure—they respond with awe and worship. All of heaven bows down and casts their crowns before the throne of God.

Praise and worship songs that focus on the great themes of Christianity and upon God Himself are primary to worship and adoration in heaven and on earth.

With this in mind, consider Brian and Anthony's song "Isn't He Great."

Isn't He Great

By Brian Johnson and Anthony Skinner

Verse 1

Isn't he great, he lights up my face
Causing worlds to shake at the sound of his name
I stood in awe when I heard him call
Out my name and I'll never be the same

Verse 2

Isn't he great, he lights up my face
Causing my world to shake
I've been touched by his grace now I am hidden in him
I've been forgiven again, I've been changed by his love
And now I'll never be the same

Chorus

Isn't he wonderful
Isn't he holy
He is the One I love
Isn't he lovely

Bridge

He became a spectacle for the world to see
I'm in love with him and he's in love with me

2nd Chorus

Isn't he wonderful today
He is the One who saves the day
The moment he came
The moment he gave
The moment he saved

Brian's song not only causes us to consider God's greatness but also includes a list of phrases that help us remember why. Remember that the list-building method is a common way to compile material for composing song sections of a worship song.

Let's use Brian's song to review the list method. Brian begins the song by asking the question, "Isn't He great?" We might answer "Yes!" but go on to develop that answer—"How is He great to you?" So, Brian begins to list some of the things that remind him of the greatness of God.

That list might look something like this:

- He lights up my face
- He shakes my world
- He calls me by name
- He changes and transforms me
- He touches me with His grace
- He hides me in Him
- He forgives me
- He changes me by His love
- He's wonderful
- He's Holy
- He's lovely
- He loves me
- He saves the day
- He suffered shame and humiliation for me

Brian and Anthony took ideas like these and built them into a song format. When composing a song around a great theme, you may want to brainstorm a list of ideas inspired by your central theme. The best ideas from your list should feel natural and be singable. We are not using the list as the song, but using the list of ideas to build the body of material.

Identify the list of ideas that help compose Brian and Jenn's song "Greatly to Be Praised."

Greatly To Be Praised

By Brian and Jenn Johnson

Song of all songs is the song we sing
Sound of all sounds heaven's symphony
Songs of love to you from us all
Songs of praise you're the One we adore

Bridge

We're gonna sing out loud
As heaven hears us and comes down
In this day that we live we'll show our love
With such awesome praise

Chorus

You are great and greatly to be praised
In all the earth, in all the earth
You are strong and powerful
In all the world, in all the heavens
You are God so wonderful
All of heaven loves your name
You are great, and greatly to be praised

*© 2004 Brian and Jenn Johnson (Admin. by Brian
Johnson, Bethel Music), CCLI# 4448938*

Now build ideas for your own worship song based on great
themes by completing the following exercises.

Practice Exercises

1)   Songs from hymnals are often already crafted around major Christian themes. Obtain old hymnals at garage and estate sales, from used bookshops, or ask to explore the storage closets of your local church. After acquiring an old hymnal, rewrite or paraphrase one or more hymns from a great theme. It is usually best to choose a hymn that you are not familiar with so that you are not bound or restricted creatively by its current melody. You may borrow a single line or an entire section of the song. Try to capture the depth of the old hymn in a fresh new way that uses as few words as possible. Watch for keyword and unique lists within the hymns that you might want to extract for your rewrite.

2)   Make a list of great themes that you would like to explore musically. You may want to compose your list from the subject index of a hymnal, topical Bible or theological workbook. After composing your list, try to come up with a hook line for each of your major themes.

3)   Write out or examine an existing list of your church's top forty worship songs. From this list identify the songs in your own worship repertoire that contain the great themes of our faith. What themes does your local church most often sing about? What themes are missing? Consider composing a praise and worship song around your church's weak or missing themes.

4)   Practice turning the messages of your local church into crafted praise and worship songs. Take notes in song form while your pastor is preaching. Share the best ones with your worship leader or in a small group for constructive feedback.

5) Choose a great theme from the category below and use the list building technique to create ideas, better defining and exploring the qualities of that theme. Use your list ideas to

compose song sections for a great theme praise and worship song.

- God as our Father
- Deity of Christ
- Trinity
- Holy Spirit
- Salvation
- The Blood
- Resurrection
- Sanctification/Holiness
- Character and Nature of God
- Love of God

Chapter Three

Personal Declarations

❧

Songs of personal declaration often overflow from the heart. Matthew 12:34 says, "...For out of the overflow of the heart the mouth speaks." In the same way, a worship writer composes from the overflow of what is in his heart.

To begin writing a personal declaration song, ask yourself questions like:

1. What do I most want to express to God today?

2. What do I sense that He wants to hear from me right now?

The answers to these questions can be the most natural source of inspiration for worship writing.

When writing a personal declaration song, it is important to remember that in any creative exercise, we must learn to suspend our critical thinking until we've had time to fully express ourselves. In other words, don't edit your song while you are first creating it. Avoid the temptation to stop and wait on a perfect rhyme or grammatical reconstruction. Make it your aim to simply catch the essence of what you want to say in its purest and rawest form. You can always enlist your critical or analytic side later to edit what you've come up with.

Sheila Davis, a well-known songwriting instructor and author of the book *The Craft of Lyric Writing* refers to this skill as "writing from both sides of your brain." Her principle is based on the theory that the right side of your brain tends to be more creative, artistic, and spontaneous while the left side is given to critical thinking, analysis, and details. The theory proposes that most people will be dominant on one side or the other. We will have a natural bend towards creative thinking or critical/analytical thinking.

The goal as a worship writer—or in any creative process— is to get the best from both sides of your brain. While I agree with much of what is taught in the left/right brain theory, I believe that one of the unique qualities of worship writing is that we are also engaging the heart and spirit as well as the intellect. Praise and worship are very much spiritual expressions often relating to feelings birthed in the depths of our heart.

The best songs of believers and pre-Christians alike come from deep places of the heart or expressions of the human spirit. Both sides of the brain are still involved in this creative process, but they are often engaged more in the refining stage than in the formative one. Using this pattern, the heart and spirit initiate the raw idea and passion for your song.

36

The moment of inspiration is a spiritual revelation, an insight, an awakening of the heart's response to the presence of God. Following the inspiration, the right brain captures appropriate phrases, pictures, and imagery; the left brain edits structure, form, rhyme, syntax and grammar. As worship writers, we want to dig deep for the kind of intimate spiritual communion that births songs awakening the heart and spirit to declare praise to God.

Songs from the heart and spirit often reflect a deep personal passion. Consider Rueben Morgan's "Lord, I Give You My Heart" and Tim Hughes' classic "Here I Am to Worship." These songs come from a deep place and call forth deep emotions within us. They make a strong declaration of praise to God that focuses as much on what we will do as upon what God has done.

Declaration of Intent

In contrast to great theme songs which focus almost entirely upon God and what He has done, personal declaration songs focus on our response to who God is for us. Great themes are God-focused adoration while this type of song focuses on our connection with God through declaration. Personal pronouns, therefore, are the identifying mark of declaration songs. A declaration song uses personal pronouns addressing yourself as "I" and God as "You." The language is personal and the focus is declarative praise to God. At first, it might seem that we are singing about ourselves, but declarative songs enforce the relational back-and-forth nature of worship. The focus is God, but with the recognition that we have a responsibility to respond to who God reveals Himself to be. This response is the essence of a personal declaration song.

Brian and Jenn Johnson have many great examples of songs declaring personal intent. Take note of the personal pronouns in the following songs:

All My Worship
By Brian Johnson

Verse

I've come here again to meet you in this place
Not just to sing aloud these songs that give you praise

Bridge

But I've come this time
To bring you something real
And I've come here now
To bring you something
All my worship

Chorus

All of me I surrender
Everything to You
All I am and all that I am to become

Chorus 2

All my worship, all my praise
All my love to you I give
All my life and all my dreams
I surrender, I surrender
All my worship, all my worship

The song "Where You Go I'll Go" is both a prayer and a personal declaration song.

Where You Go I'll Go

By Brian Johnson, and Jon Mohr

Chorus

Where you go I go
What you say I say
What you pray I pray
What you pray I pray

Verse

Jesus only did what he saw you do
He would only say what he heard you speak
He would only move when he felt you lead
Following your heart, following your Spirit

Pre-Chorus

How could I expect to walk without you
When every move that Jesus made was in surrender
I will not begin to live without you
For you alone are worthy and you are always good

Bridge

Though the world sees and soon forgets
We will not forget who you are
And what you've done for us

The song "I Will Bless Your Name" is a specific response to the greatness of God. It has a powerful duel focus of presenting God's greatness in the verse and then making a personal declaration in response. What makes this song a declaration rather than a description or great theme song, is that the song hook (or chorus) section focuses on the personal declaration.

Many songs look like they could actually fit in several categories of song types. The defining feature of any song is the song hook, because it carries the main lyrical and musical idea of the song in one short phrase.

I Will Bless Your Name

By Brian Johnson

Mighty God you reign in all the earth
Awesome King displayed in majesty
High above the kingdoms of the world
You alone have won my heart

Chorus

So I will bless your name
With everything in me I give you praise
For you are great and how worthy is your name
I will bless your name

Verse 2

Holy One your life has shown me the way
Through your Son the greatest debt has been paid
Now in turn I give you all that I am
For you alone have won my heart

Bridge

Amazing grace how sweet the sound
That saved someone like me
When I was lost you sent Your Son
His blood ran down for me

Lamentations

Another type of song that is inspired and requires a personal declaration is a song of lamentation. Author and prophet Graham Cooke has said that lamentation is the highest form of praise because it is purely motivated by faith.

King David penned many lamentation praise songs in the Bible. These songs express an honest overflow from a heart that is searching for answers.

> *How long, O LORD? Will you forget me forever? How long will you hide your face from me? How long must I wrestle with my thoughts and every day have sorrow in my heart? How long will my enemy triumph over me?* (Psalm 13:1-2)

Now notice the personal declaration of praise that comes out of these hard and painful questions:

> *But I trust in your unfailing love; my heart rejoices in your salvation* (v. 5).

David's song explores the depths of human pain, suffering, and even spiritual questions like "Where is God when I'm suffering?" The key to this psalm is that David's lyrics don't leave us in the dark places. Lamentation songs identify with the darkness we all experience but end by refocusing us on the unchanging goodness of God. Out of that place we make a strong declaration of praise, "I will trust..."

A classic example of a lamentation can be found in Matt Redman's declaration "Blessed Be Your Name." In this song Matt calls for praise from the desert places, the wilderness, and the road of suffering. Darrell Evan's bridge on "Trading My Sorrows" carries the Apostle Paul's lament of being "pressed...but not crushed...persecuted...not abandoned, struck down but not destroyed" (2 Corinthians 4:8-10).

Lamentation songs ask hard questions and look at tough situations. These songs encourage us to explore the dark places that are real to all human beings. The truth and honesty of these songs pull us in and then help us to bring a fitting sacrifice of praise even when we don't fully understand our circumstance.

Don't be afraid to explore some of the dark places we worship from; but remember not to leave us there. If you choose to meet your listener in a dark place, then be sure to bring them out to a true declaration of praise and worship.

One of the classic lamentations composed out of pain and sorrow is Horatio Spafford's "It is Well With My Soul."

> *"This hymn was written after two major traumas in Spafford's life. The first was the great Chicago Fire of October 1871 which ruined him financially (he had been a wealthy businessman). Shortly after, while crossing the Atlantic, all four of Spafford's daughters died in a collision with another ship. Spafford's wife Anna survived and sent him the now famous telegram, "Saved alone." Several weeks later, as Spafford's own ship passed near the spot where his daughters died, the Holy Spirit inspired these words. They speak to the eternal hope that all believers have, no matter what pain and grief befall them on earth."[12]*

It Is Well with My Soul

Words by Horatio G. Spafford, Music by Philip P. Bliss

When peace, like a river, attendeth my way,
When sorrows like sea billows roll;

Whatever my lot, Thou hast taught me to say,
It is well, it is well with my soul.

Refrain

It is well with my soul,
It is well, it is well with my soul.

Though Satan should buffet,
Though trials should come,
Let this blest assurance control,
That Christ has regarded my helpless estate,
And hath shed His own blood for my soul.

My sin, oh, the bliss of this glorious thought!
My sin, not in part but the whole,
Is nailed to the cross, and I bear it no more,
Praise the Lord, praise the Lord, O my soul!

And, Lord, haste the day when my faith shall be sight,
The clouds be rolled back as a scroll;
The trump shall resound, and the Lord shall descend,
Even so, it is well with my soul.
© *Public Domain*

Robert Critchley, of the Toronto Airport Christian Fellowship, composed a fantastic song of praise following the loss of his newborn son, Caleb. The song is called "What a Faithful God." Written in the same spirit of faith as Spafford's hymn, composed over one hundred years earlier, Rob declares the faithfulness of God in the midst of a painful situation.

Remember that a lamentation song—while exploring the questions, problems, trials and difficulties of life—never leave us in the dark. This is where the declaration comes in. A lamentation is a declaration of our intent or of God's identity.

The writer's declaration of intent can be expressed by words like, "Yet, I will…" or "It is well with my soul." A declaration of God's identity would be, "Blessed be the name of the Lord" or "Yet, He is faithful."

Lamentations use the powerful song-building tool of contrast. In a lamentation song, the problem or question is contrasted with our response or revelation of God. Contrasting lyrical ideas, rhythms, and musical sections keep a song interesting. Intentional use of contrast is a strong compositional tool.

Songs of Repentance

Declaration songs can also be expressions of repentance or dedication. Matt Redman's song "Heart of Worship" is a confession of both repentance and praise. Singing songs of repentance are a fitting form of praise and worship, especially when they are combined with a declaration of praise.

Whether you're writing from a passionate connection with God or a place of heartache or repentance, the challenge for writers of these deeply personal songs is to maintain a universal theme. The song should be something that everyone can relate to, even if they have not personally had the same experience.

Inexperienced writers often plunge deep into personal experiences expressed with vague imagery that leaves the listener wondering what they're talking about. Esoteric phrases and experiences are not in themselves deep or moving. If you want to write a song that has a broader audience than yourself, then find a declaration of praise that everyone can relate to.

Use the following exercises to sharpen your skills in writing a personal declaration song.

Practice Exercises

1)   Identify two or three popular worship songs that you would consider to be a personal declaration. Look for deeply personal themes using first-person pronouns. Write out the lyrics taking note of what makes these songs strong.

2)   Take time to answer these questions presented earlier in the lesson.

- What do I most want to express to God?

- What does God most want to hear from my heart right now?

Write a hook line that represents your answer to these questions.

3)   Start the composition of a lamentation by considering questions you have about your life or about God.

- What things might seem in contrast to praise? Contrast verses that speak from the dark places of life with a heart of praise.

- Construct a chorus that expresses praise in the midst of difficult situations.

Chapter Four

Vicarious Voices

❧

In the last lesson, we explored writing from our own heart and experiences. This lesson will focus on helping us give musical expression to the voice of others. "Vicarious voices" refers to writing on behalf of someone else. The word "vicarious" literally means "serving in stead of someone or something else; an experience realized through imaginative or sympathetic participation in the experience of others."

This form of songwriting is often intercessory in nature

because it explores the heart cry of others and then brings it before the Lord as if it were the writer's own personal offering of praise.

Voice of the Local Church

One of the voices that must find musical expression is the voice of your local church. Brian Doerksen gives worship writers this charge:

> *"Seek to give musical language to the heart of your congregation."*[13]

Consider songs like "We Are Hungry" by Brad Kilman, and "We Fall Down" by Chris Tomlin. These songs give voice to the larger community of believers and remind us that we are part of a great Body of worshipers.

This song differs from a personal declaration by using the corporate pronoun "we." Typically, this corporate declaration will either be a statement of intent or identity. Declarations of intent speak of what we will do, are doing, or have done. Corporate declarations of identity speak to who we are.

The song "We Believe" by Brian Johnson is a declaration of the voice of his local church as well as a growing number of churches that have partnered together for revival. Brian's song is a corporate declaration of intent because it makes statements like "we believe," "we will ascend," and "we will stand." These corporate declarations help the local church to position itself in a place of unified response to the greatness of what God is doing.

We Believe
By Brian Johnson

Verse

You reveal your secrets and all your mysteries
To those who have fallen completely in love with you

Bridge

We believe in your Son and the power of the cross
We believe in your blood and what you did for us
We believe in your Kingdom, your Kingdom has come
Here on the earth will of God be done

Chorus

We will ascend your holy mountain
We will stand in your presence and speak to the winds
Eyes have not seen what you have for us Lord
Ears have not heard what you have
For those who believe

Voice of Creation

Finding the heart cry of your local church is only one of the voices that must find musical language. In her famous worship chorus "Shout to the Lord," Darlene Zschech gives a musical voice to all of creation and invites the rest of us to sing along. To me, Darlene's song captures the voice of creation that is expressed in Psalm nineteen.

> *The heavens declare the glory of God; the skies proclaim the work of his hands. Day after day they pour forth speech; night after night they display knowledge. There*

is no speech or language where their voice is not heard (vs. 1-3).

This theme, focused on the voice of creation, is in no way exhausted. Lamont Hibbert's song "Ocean" is another song that expresses the voice of creation praising God.

What else do you hear creation crying out? Mankind was originally given stewardship over creation in the Garden of Eden.

> *Then God said, "Let us make man in our image, in our likeness, and let them rule over the fish of the sea and the birds of air, over the livestock, over all the earth, and over all the creatures that move along the ground"* (Genesis 1:26).

The book of Romans expresses the idea that all of creation is groaning and travailing, waiting for something from the sons of God.

> *The creation waits in eager expectation for the sons of God to be revealed. For the creation was subjected to frustration, not by its own choice, but by the will of the one who subjected it, in hope that the creation itself will be liberated from its bondage to decay and brought into the glorious freedom of the children of God* (Romans 8:19-21).

Mankind is still a steward of the earth, a mediator between what is possible in heaven and what is manifest on earth. Many psalms and other portions of Scripture call for creation to praise the Lord. One of the ways we can give voice to creation is to write using the imagery and metaphors that relate to our specific geography. If you live by the ocean, then ask yourself what the ocean is declaring about the glory and greatness of God. In a mountainous region, it's great to compose local worship songs that give a voice to the mountains. In a rural farming area, you may want to write about the waving fields or fruitful plains. Even the desert cries out for rain.

Consider writing worship songs that give a specific voice to the geographical features of your region. Doing so accomplishes many things. First of all, geographical and topographical metaphors from nature are easily understood and can be related to by your local congregation. Giving language to creation in your local region connects people with a healthy stewardship and pride in the land God has given them. I believe that giving a voice to the creation of your local region also connects it with heaven's possibilities. When we link heaven and earth through the bridge of the voice of man, powerful things happen.

> *For since the creation of the world God's invisible qualities—his eternal power and divine nature—have been clearly seen, being understood from what has been made, so that men are without excuse* (Romans 1:20).

What is the voice of your local region? What is creation around you declaring about God's glory, power, and nature that you can give voice to?

Voice of the Lost and Brokenhearted

Worship songs can also give expression to the brokenhearted and the weary. Songs like Brenton Brown's "All Who Are Thirsty" and Don Moen's "God Will Make a Way" encourage the worshipers to focus on the greatness and faithfulness of God rather than their own circumstance.

I think that Brian Johnson's song "We Cry Out" captures

an intercessory voice for the lost and broken in our nation.

We Cry Out

By Brian Johnson

Verse

Oh Lord we cry out we've been lost
We need your mercies Oh God
We repent for our ways and we turn to you again

Oh Lord we cry out we've been lost
Change our hearts to yours Oh God
We repent for our sin and we turn to you again

Chorus

Oh God we cry out for your mercy
Oh God we cry out for your grace
Oh God we cry out set us free
Oh God we cry out once again, once again

© 1996 Brian Johnson (Admin. by Brian Johnson, Bethel Music), CCLI# 4405579

Consider writing a song expressing the voice of a specific demographic group in your region. What are people crying out for in your region? What would the prayer of lost or hurting people in your community be? Give voice to their cry as an intercessory and compassionate act.

Voice of a Generation

In our worship writing schools, we want students to see themselves as musical intercessors who lift up the voices of the lost, the broken-hearted, the weary, the church, and even of a nation. What if you could capture the cry of your generation so vividly in song that you gave a voice of praise to an entire generation?

Plato, student of Socrates and mentor of Aristotle, is quoted as saying:

> *"Give me the songs of a generation and I will change the mind of that generation."*

Blaise Pascal was a child prodigy who pioneered realms of science, physics, and mathematics in the seventeenth century. Pascal said:

> *"The people who have the greatest influence in shaping the hearts and minds of any generation are not the folks who write the laws, but those who write the songs."*

Bill Johnson gives the Bethel School of Worship students each year a mandate to write songs about what they want to see in the next five to ten years. Don't just write about what you already have. We believe that words can shape worlds and music can transform mindsets. If you only sing about what you have seen and experienced, then you may limit your own experience. Write about what you want to see and experience in the days to come.

With this understanding Brian wrote a song that I believe expresses the desire of a generation seeking revival.

Revival Generation

By Brian Johnson

Verse 1

I heard an old man talking of a time

That was long ago he said
The fire's been dormant for awhile but he was praying
And with this prayer my heart caught fire
And now it won't let go
'Cause I found the reason why I'm alive

Verse 2

We're a new breed rising and we're coming
We're gonna take a stand
There is a new passion burning in our hearts
A new love for Jesus a new hope and a vision
For this revival here we are

Chorus

It's revival time
We are a revival generation
It's revival time
We are a revival generation

Verse 3

Consecrated is who we are
It's who we're called to be
We'd rather see revival than build these kingdoms
Of pride and greed
Fan into flame this revival fire let it burn
Crush your children until our hearts are inflamed

© 1997 Brian Johnson (Admin. by Brian Johnson, Bethel Music), CCLI# 4029625

Voice of the Lord

Zephaniah chapter three reveals an amazing thing about God.

The LORD your God is with you, he is mighty to save. He will take great delight in you, he will quiet you with His love, he will rejoice over you with singing" (v. 17).

Did you see it? God rejoices over us with singing. God literally sings songs over us.

Sometimes in praise and worship we need to give voice to what God is saying or singing over us. These songs are powerful reminders of His heart and perspective towards us and can create an atmosphere of nearness, deliverance, and healing.

Brian Johnson crafted a chorus around giving voice to the Lord in the song "Broken For You."

Broken For You

By Brian Johnson

Chorus
Oh, I sleep but my heart is awake
It's the voice of the One that I love
He's crying, "Will you open to me
My love, my perfect one."

© *1996 Brian Johnson (Admin. by Brian Johnson, Bethel Music), CCLI# 4405706*

Another of Brian Johnson's songs that gives us a perspective on how God is thinking and feeling about us is found in "You Have Ravished My Heart." This entire song is sung from the Lord to His Bride.

You Have Ravished My Heart

By Brian Johnson

Verse 1

I will draw you to me forever
In righteousness in justice and in mercy
No longer your master
But your husband I will be

Chorus

You have ravished my heart
With one glance of your eyes
How fair is your love
My promised, my bride

Verse 2

I will draw you to me forever
In lovingkindess, in faithfulness and grace
No longer your master
But your husband I will be

One of my favorite songs from the category of the voice of the Lord is the turnaround chorus in Jenn Johnson's song entitled "A Little Longer." Jenn starts the song in a personal voice asking what she can do to please God, and then she crafts the chorus to be God's response of grace and passion.

A Little Longer

By Jenn Johnson

What can I do for you

What can I bring to you
What kind of song would you like me to sing
I'll dance a dance for you
Pour out my love to you
What can I do for you beautiful King

Chorus

'Cause I can't thank You enough
I can't thank you enough

Then I hear you sing to me
You don't have to do a thing
Just simply be with me and let those things go
'Cause they can wait another minute
Wait, this moment is too sweet,
Would you please stay here, here with me
And love on me a little longer
'Cause I'm in love with you

Writing songs in the voice of the Lord reminds us that He is singing over us as well. Worship, like prayer, should be a two-way communication. Songs from God's perspective can be a strong draw to a greater awareness of our divine union and intimacy with God.

Give yourself to the following exercises to practice writing in the voices of various groups of people.

Practice Exercises

Take time to prayerfully consider what you believe to be the unique cry of the following groups. Write out your answers. Work at crafting each of these cries over time into a song of praise and worship.

• **Your local church.** Ask, "What is our corporate identity? What is a declaration we need to make to the Lord? Is there a specific area we should be committing ourselves to?

• **The brokenhearted the lost and weary.** God is near to the brokenhearted and poor in spirit. What does that look like in your community? What is the cry of the poor? What areas of injustice might be addressed in a song?

• **A specific demographic group like children, young people, senior citizens, couples, singles, divorced, etc.** Is there anything unique to how they would voice their praises? What would their praises sound like musically?

• **Your nation, culture, or geographical region in creation. What are unique aspects of your geographical region?** What do these elements in creation speak about the glory, power, or nature of God? How might you represent these in a song?

• **The voice of the Lord over you.** What do you think God is singing over you right now? What is He singing over your church or your city? Ask Him. Take time to meditate on His answer and listen for His song.

Chapter Five

Prayers and Petitions

❧

Prayers and praises are inseparably intertwined throughout the Word of God. Most of David's psalms were as much a prayer as they were a song of praise. In the book of Revelation, prayers are represented as bowls and praises as harps.

And when he had taken it,

the four living creatures and the twenty-four elders fell down before the Lamb. Each one had a harp and they were holding golden bowls full of incense, which are the prayers of the saints. And they sang a new song... (Revelation 5:8-9a).

Together the prayers and praises rise like incense before the throne of God. Singing prayers has proven powerful in both heaven and earth. Paul the apostle makes a declaration that seems to link praying and singing as a regular part of his devotional exercise.

> *So what shall I do? I will pray with my spirit, but I will also pray with my mind; I will sing with my spirit, but I will also sing with my mind* (1 Corinthians 14:15).

Many of the songs we sing in church today are actually prayers. Brian Doerksen had a popular prayer song a few years ago combining a prayer with Scripture in "Light the Fire Again." This is a powerful prayer for revival and the passion of first love for the Lord. The popular Paul Baloche song "Open the Eyes of My Heart" is another Scripture-based prayer that has had a long impact on the church. Tim Hughes is another modern writer who has impacted nations with prayer songs like "Consuming Fire."

Prayer and Worship Movements

Singing prayers have often been the fuel for mighty moves of God. Mike Bickle, director of the International House of Prayer Missions Base of Kansas City (IHOP-KC), has been pioneering a spiritual exploration of the "harp and bowl" model of prayer and worship. Twenty-four hours a day for more than thirteen years, IHOP in Kansas City has been lifting non-stop prayers and praises before the Lord. Musicians, singers, and prayer leaders work in shifts and teams so that they can follow the heavenly pattern of unceasing praises before God.

A similar movement has flourished in England's youth culture where they have established "Boiler Rooms" or

"Prayer Furnaces" with a similar pattern of sustained prayer and praise.

Historically, whenever a people gave themselves to a continual discipline of praise and prayer, revival and reformation followed. Examples of this can be studied from the time of David's tabernacle in Israel throughout the Celtic and Moravian communities that influenced the entire evangelization of Europe. Singing prayers is not only biblically and historically documented, it also seems to be a great catalyst for spiritual transformation.

Allen Ganta was a young worship leader for a congregation of twenty-six people that met in the basement of a rented Catholic church in Hyderabad, India. Allen came to one of our songwriting schools in America and learned that he could write musical prayers for his nation. Upon returning to India, Allen was invited to sing his prayer over a gathering of forty-thousand believers in Mumbai. Today, Allen is one of the most popular worship writers in his people group.

Here is the prayer Allen penned for his nation.

Open the Windows of Heaven

By Allen Ganta

Let your glory come
Let your fire fall
Like a sweet-smelling fragrance
All across this nation
Lord, we seek your face
We repent of our ways
So hear our cry from heaven
Come and heal this land

Chorus

Open the windows of heaven
Pour out a blessing across this nation
Lord, we're waiting for
Something more from you
We're waiting Lord

© *Allen Ganta, Sounds of the Nations India*

Brian and Jenn Johnson have also been part of a national prayer movement filling stadiums at "The Call" events with Lou Engle. We've already mentioned their song "We Cry Out" in the last chapter in reference to giving a vicarious voice to the lost generation in America.

Another powerful prayer song of Brian's is a prayer for believers to go higher in their experience with God entitled "Day unto Day."

Day unto Day

By Brian Johnson

Day unto day you utter forth
Night unto night I listen for your voice
Off in my dreams your spirit speaks
Unveiled mysteries come speak to me

Bridge

Take me away with you
Take me where eagles fly
I want to see your face

Take me away with you
Take me where eagles fly
I want to hear your voice
Your Spirit calls to take me higher

Chorus
Take me higher
Take me higher

Writing a Prayer Song

So, how do you start writing a prayer song? Similar to the psalming exercise we studied early, it is often helpful to start by simply singing your prayers and petitions to the Lord during your regular times of prayer.

I find that adding melodies to my prayers involves more of my whole person in the prayer. My petitions become more passionate and focused.

When I sing my prayers, it is less likely that thoughts or imaginations will cause distractions than when I only use words.

I sing my prayers in freeform without trying to rhyme words, pair lines, or match melodic phrases. Often my heart will catch a specific line or phrase that I am drawn to repeat several times.

If I hit on something powerful or meaningful, I quickly write down any lines or record the melodies that seem to carry me closer to the Lord. Later, I apply the craft of songwriting to this raw material and shape it into an appropriate song form.

Whenever you find a line that sings well and seems to carry you somewhere in the Spirit, consider crafting it into a song hook. Remember from the first chapter that a song hook is the part of the song that expresses the main idea of the song in as few notes and words as possible. The song hook is often the title of the song. A song hook can also be repeated lyrically and musically within the chorus section.

The main line from your prayer still may need some crafting to be an effective song hook. Here are a few suggestions on how to turn a great song idea into a catchy song hook.

A Well-Stated Phrase

A song hook can just be a well-stated phrase. It should be clear, concise, and clever. The song hook should be something everyone can relate to but said in a way that is fresh and interesting. An example could be seen in Ben Fielding and Rueben Morgan's song, "Mighty to Save." It is concise, clear, something we can all relate to, but it is well-said and fresh.

Often it is good to write down a longer version of exactly what you want to say and then cross out every unnecessary word until you get the most concise form of your original sentence. Then go back to your shortened sentence and replace every weak word with something more powerful or descriptive. The fewer words the better. The average song hook on CCLI's charts of top twenty-five songs sung in churches in America is less than four words long (3.44 to be exact!). The shortest song hook is one word; the longest is seven words.

Keep your song hook as clear and concise as possible.

Alliteration and Assonance

Many song hooks also use the mnemonic device of alliteration or assonance. This simply means that several of the words begin with the same letter. The worship classic, "How Great is our God" by Chris Thomlin, is an example of the repeating G-sound. "Blessed be Your Name" by Matt and Beth Redman uses the repeated B-sound. "Above All" by Lenny LeBlanc and Paul Baloche repeats the A-sound. This type of simple sound repetition, when used tastefully, can make a song hook more memorable.

Contrasting ideas

Another simple way of building song hooks is through two contrasting ideas. Joel Houston sings about loving God "From the Inside Out." The contrast of in-and-out make the song hook memorable and intriguing. Using contrasting ideas to form a song hook is also employed in Brenton Brown's song "Humble King."

Practice Exercises

1)   Over the next two weeks, try singing popular prayer songs as a part of your regular devotional time. As you sing these songs, be careful to sing them from the heart as a prayer and not just a catchy melody.

Repeat phrases that seem to carry you closer to God. Take your liberty in adding your own words or altering melodies and tempos. This practice will introduce you to the power that is released while singing prayers.

2)   After taking a few weeks to practice devotional singing with current prayer songs, begin to sing your own prayers and petitions. Avoid the temptation to put them in song structures while you are praying.

- Use free verse and association to sing around a theme from different perspectives.

- Experiment with repeating phrases that seem to carry you somewhere.

- After the prayer time, write or record any ideas that seem to have the breath of the Spirit on them. Try repeating these ideas in subsequent prayer times and see if they have the same or intensified effect.

- If a prayer song consistently draws you to a deeper place, take the time to craft it into a form that others can enjoy with you.

- Try sharing it first in a small group setting or prayer meeting. If it proves effective there, then you may want to share it in a larger public setting.

Chapter Six

Songs of Invocation

Invocation songs are those that invite an individual or congregation into a specific action of praise. Often the invitation will include attributes of God that inspire that specific response. King David often used invocations to draw people into worship.

> *Come, let us bow down in worship, let us kneel before the LORD our Maker; for he is our God and we are the people of his pasture, the flock under his care* (Psalm 95:6-7).

Clap your hands, all you nations; shout to God with cries of joy. How awesome is the LORD Most High, the great King over all the earth! (Psalm 47:1-2)

Take note of the fact that each invocation contains both an invitational element and an attribute that relates to the invitation. As is true in other forms of worship writing, be careful to make a single, clear invitation to the worshiper. Before composing a song of invocation, the writer should have a definite sense of what they want to call forth and why.

The two parts of an invocation song are the invitation and the reason. In Psalm 95 we are invited to come and bow and kneel before God because He is our God and we are His people. In Psalm 47 we are invited to clap our hands and shout because God is awesome and the great King over all the earth.

Often I have seen worship leaders cheerleading the congregation. They tell everyone to stand and shout and are given the reason: "If you were in a sporting event, you would be clapping and cheering with all of your heart." The truth is, fans only clap and cheer when something exciting happens on the field—there is an event that inspires such an enthusiastic response.

The difference between exhorting a congregation and "hyping" the crowd is inspiration. When we ask people to do something without reminding them why, then it often becomes a religious form devoid of true worship. A great invocation song will invite people to worship God in a distinct way, but it will also inspire that response through pointing to something God has done or to an aspect of His character and nature that is worthy of that response.

I remember a worship service where we were singing the Chris Thomlin song, "How Great is Our God." The congregation seemed tired and the song had all the energy of a funeral dirge. All of a sudden I remembered that one of the members of the congregation had just been healed of stage four terminal cancer. I invited him to the platform to testify. The crowd cheered with delight at the testimony of this great healing. When the band started back into the song, "How Great is Our God," it was an explosion of authentic praise. That's the power of singing with revelation and understanding. This story also demonstrates the importance of revelation and reason in a good invocation song.

The Doxology is another example of a song of invocation.

The Doxology

By Thomas Ken

Praise God from whom all blessings flow
Praise him all creatures here below
Praise him above ye heavenly host
Praise Father, Son, and Holy Ghost
Amen.

Words by Thomas Ken, 1674, Public Domain

Notice that the first line includes both aspects of a strong song of invocation. First, there is the invitation to "Praise God..." Secondly, it lists the attribute that inspires us to praise Him, "From whom all blessings flow." His blessings are one of the many things about God that inspire us to thank, praise, and worship Him.

An invocation song can call forth and inspire any biblical form of praise, such as clapping, dancing, jumping, bowing, shouting, or being still and silent before God.

I really enjoy Brian's invocation song "Come Everyone," because it is a call to both heaven and earth to join in praising the goodness of God.

69

Come Everyone

By Brian Johnson

Come everyone let's gather together
And sing the song of the Lamb
Come every angel from the highest of heaven
Sing to the great I AM
Come every nation come every tongue
Lift up your voices in praise
Come all creation all in one voice
Sing out your praises to Him

Chorus

For he is a good God, he is a great God
His love will endure throughout every generation
We will be planted by the river all the days of our lives
And it will be well with our souls
It will be well with our souls

Chorus 2

For you are a good God
You are a great God
Your love will endure throughout every generation
We will be planted by the river
All the days of our lives
And it will be well with our souls
It will be well with our souls

Where to Use Invocation Songs

The value of songs of invocation in congregational worship is significant. Used at the front of a service they often help members of the congregation to enter into a specific expression of worship.

> *Enter His gates with thanksgiving and his courts with praise; give thanks to him and praise his name* (Psalm 100:4).

This has been the value of songs like Brian Doerksen's "Come, Now is the Time to Worship." It is often used to remind people of how significant our worship is in this season. Songs of invocation can also be used to transition us into a new or deeper place of worship expression later in a song set.

Bible scholars estimate that there are over 1,200 invitations in Scripture and more than 50 expressions of praise. With this much biblical support, there should be no end to the effective invocation songs we can compose for the church. Now that you understand the basic elements of an invocation song, let's practice.

71

Practice Exercises

1) Study the following Scripture sections that employ an invocation. For each Psalm, write out what the invitation is and what the attributes are that inspire that particular action.

- Psalm 33
- Psalm 47
- Psalm 66
- Psalm 95

Experiment with setting one of these scriptural invocations to original music.

2) The key to a strong invocation song is in presenting the attributes that stir that specific response. For each of the following biblical forms of praise answer the question, "What things about God make me want to respond this way?"

- Lift my hands
- Clap my hands
- Bow down
- Dance

Take your strongest ideas and craft them into a song of invocation.

3) Take note of what biblical expressions of worship are least common in your local worship service. Craft an invocation song that invites people to express their praise and worship in that specific manner. Be sure to include reasons or attributes that inspire that particular response.

Chapter Seven

Heaven's Download

꙰

The "heavenly download" is what I call a song idea that comes to you all at once. It is like the music and lyrics just pop up into your heart. When this happens, it is important to write it down or record it as soon as possible. These kinds of songs often leave as quickly as they come. Many times I have been lazy and thinking the idea is so catchy that there was no way I would forget it—only to lose the idea later. Songwriters should always carry around an idea pad or notebook (often called a "hook book") to capture song ideas as they come. If possible, it is also a good idea to keep a recording device at hand. Many cell phones have the ability to record.

The worship song "I Love You Lord" came as a heavenly download to Laurie Klein back in 1974. She described it as "a gift from God that appeared spontaneously."[14] After the words and music came for the first two phrases of the song, she decided to get a pen and write it down. When Laurie came back with the writing utensils, the second two phrases came just as easily. It was six years before the song surfaced on a Maranatha! Music album, but since that time, it has spent many years in the top twenty-five worship songs sung around the world.

There are two ideas that I have found prevalent among worship writers regarding heavenly download songs.

1. Some believe that we should only write songs that are downloaded in our spirit from God. Learning the craft of songwriting is, therefore, not necessary.

2. Some writers believe that when we receive a download from heaven, we should never touch or change any part of it because it came from God, and is, therefore, "holy."

Creativity

Every believer must live by their own conviction on these things, but, generally speaking, I think both of these concepts represent wrong ideas about God. First of all, if we only brought God the songs He has downloaded to us, then we could never bring a sacrifice of praise. I see Christianity as an equal balance between God's sovereignty and man's responsibility. God created man in His own image so that man might also be creative.

Our creativity is a reflection of His glory and divine nature in our lives. Only man—among all created things—has the ability to improve upon an idea. Birds have always built nests, but they are not building two-room condos out of plywood and renting them to other birds. Beavers have not improved upon their original design by using concrete instead of wood to build their homes and dams. Mankind, however, is always attempting a new thing in a new way.

The gift of creativity and variety is one of the fingerprints of God upon our lives. We should use these creative gifts to craft the things that God has dropped into our hearts.

Secondly, some are afraid to craft or reshape a lyric that seems to have come from God. Once again, I have several problems with this line of thinking. The only completely inerrant revelation given to us from God is His written Word, the Bible. God is still speaking to His servants today, but our hearing is not yet perfected. Even prophetic words we receive from the Holy Spirit are "knowing in part and prophesying in part."[15] Therefore, all that we receive from God is subject to our human frailties and should be carefully tested and weighed.

When considering this issue, it is wise to look at the parable of the talents.[16] One servant who was given a single talent was afraid to invest it because he misunderstood the nature of his master. When the master returned, he was angry with the "wicked" servant who had no increase to show from what was given him to invest. The "wicked" servant was fearful to touch or change what had been given to him. Does this sound familiar? In the spirit of stewardship it seems to me that we should take what we have been given from the Master and make the most we can out of it.

John Barnett with Vineyard Music warns us to resist the urge to "canonize" our songs.

> *"Sometimes we want to canonize the songs we write... 'This is the way God gave it to me and therefore it stands. Don't mess with it. Do not change it. Do not play it any other way.'"*[17]

Brian Doerksen put it this way:

> *"Many times when songwriters are insecure they will hide behind spiritual words and imply that God is on their side by saying, 'God gave me this song.' I think it is far better to share the song and have someone else say, 'Wow, that really touched me; God must have inspired you to write that.'"*[18]

Now, I am definitely not saying that God cannot give us a song in finished form. Often He does! I am merely suggesting that we are not to assume that a song is complete until we have subjected it to the same tests and scrutiny as songs that come from other sources of inspiration.

Jeffery Steele was considered one of the hottest songwriters of his day in Nashville with over two hundred cuts on the charts in only three years' time. Jeffery says of his own songwriting:

> *"Occasionally, I get struck by lightning. You all know that it is few and far between when you get that zap— 'Oh my God, I've got a great idea...!' You do what you do every day, so when you do get struck by that occasional bolt of lightning, you've got your craft together and you know where to chase it."*[19]

So, songwriting is not a competition between the heavenly download and hard work; rather, it should be both a matter of inspiration and perspiration. Let the aspiring worship writer not be lazy in either pursuit.

Let's chase after God for creative inspiration and that download from heaven. And, let us also apply wisdom and crafting to what He has given us, so that we might offer it back to Him as a sacrifice of praise.

Matt Redman says:

> *"I really encourage worship leaders to get on their knees and get into hard work as well and write some worship songs."*[20]

Practice Exercises

1) Spontaneous singing is a great way to develop sensitivity for heavenly downloads. Find a chord progression or instrumental bed that moves you, and then sing spontaneous lyrics as they come to you.

Take time to tune your heart to God in prayer and meditation of his Word so that God will have raw material to draw from.

Consider the words of the Prophet Habakkuk:

> *I will stand at my watch and station myself on the ramparts; I will look to see what he will say to me, and what answer I am to give to this complaint. Then the LORD replied: "Write down the revelation and make it plain on tablets so that a herald may run with it.*

> *For the revelation awaits an appointed time; it speaks of the end and will not prove false. Though it linger, wait for it; it will certainly come and will not delay"* (2:1-3).

Now answer the following questions:

• How is the servant of the Lord to position himself to hear from God?

• What is the servant to do with what God has given him?

• How soon will God use what He has given you? Is your revelation always for this immediate time period?

78

2)   Expect that God will speak to you anytime of the day or night as you go through your normal life routine. Keep a note pad, pen, and recording device with you to demonstrate your faith and desire for God to speak to you. Keep a journal of your inspired ideas and shape these ideas with patience waiting for their "appointed time."

I have had song ideas that did not take their final form until many years later. Sometimes a song vision comes as a promise of things to come much later.

Be patient and persistent with your song ideas. Give your vision and inspiration time to grow and mature. Great songs often take shape over time.

Chapter Eight

Song Doctor Rewriting Tips

Have you ever completed a song and the next morning not felt the same breath on it? "Wow, yesterday, I loved this song, and today, it just lacks something." Or, have you ever been excited about a song, but when you play it for a friend or family member, they smile politely and say, "That's nice."

It's a terrible feeling to lose your first love for a song you have written, but it happens to every songwriter.

In this chapter we will examine some rewriting and revision tools for improving your song ideas.

One Great Idea

Great songs start with one great idea. Remember that a worship song is not a three-point sermon or a Sunday School lesson.

Consider if your song qualifies by using the following criteria:

- Is the idea something that moves you?
- Are you passionate about the subject?
- Is there a clear, concise, well-stated song hook?

Many songs take you for a walk, but not a journey. A walk has no particular destination, but a journey has the destination in mind. Make sure that you have a destination in mind while crafting your song.

Go back and examine your song with the following questions in mind:

- Are there any competing ideas?

- Does everything in your song focus on building and featuring the song hook?

If not, rewrite any line that competes with the hook. If the hook is weak, then try rewriting the song hook several times until you have the strongest representation of what you want to say musically and lyrically.

One Voice

Many novice worship writers change the pronoun tense in their songs. In the verse section they may refer to God as

"He," while in the chorus section they refer to God as "You."

You must choose one point of view and stick with it. As you are writing your song, ask yourself:

- Is this a personal tense song (singing to God)?
- Is this a declaration song (singing about God)?

Both tenses are great use, but you must choose one tense and stick with it consistently throughout the song.

I have also seen beginning worship writers bounce back and forth between "I" and "we." So, ask yourself: is this a personal or corporate declaration?

Decide which tense to use before writing your song, and the result will be clearer and more satisfying.

Rhyme Abuse

Songwriting is not poetry writing. Over-rhyming can sometimes be a problem with beginning writers. Obvious rhymes like "me, tree, and free" can kill an otherwise great song idea.

Generally speaking, you don't want to rhyme every line. Any great interior designer will tell you that you can't decorate a room by throwing all the pieces you like into one room. Rather, you must choose a color scheme and a theme for each room.

In the same way, rhymes should have a scheme. Usually the rhyme scheme appears as first and third or second and forth line pairs. You should use the same rhyme scheme for every matching song section but different or no rhyme scheme for complimentary sections.

For instance, if you rhyme the second and fourth line of two verses, use no rhyme scheme for the chorus. If you rhyme on a bridge, then use a first and third line rhyme scheme.

These variations will help prevent rhyme abuse and the outcome will be a much more pleasing song that everyone will enjoy.

Too Many Words

The average number of unique lines in a popular worship song is eight to twelve. Most novice writers use too many words to describe what they want to say.

If you have a great line, consider putting it in a place where you can repeat it. Simple, well-written songs stand the test of time, because, they are not only easy to sing, but also easy to remember. If your song has too many words, then go through and identify your favorite lines. Cross out every word in your song that does not absolutely need to be there. And finally, see if there is a much simpler way to say a particular line in your song.

Try rewriting your song using only your favorite lines and the words necessary to connect them in a logical order.

Avoid using filler words that force a rhyme, or just complete the timing of your word cadence. Make every word count and you will definitely enjoy your songs more.

Too Many Sections

Another error of novice writers is to have too many song sections. If you envision your song being sung in a church service, then consider the person running the lyrics on the screens. The popular average number of song sections for a worship song is three—verse, chorus, and bridge. Too many refrains, pre-choruses, second choruses, and vamps can crowd the memorable quality of your song and challenge its singability.

If you come up with more than three song sections that you love, then consider splitting some off into a new song. Too many great lines or song sections can leave us asking questions like, "Which section is the chorus?" or, "What is the song hook?"

Keep to a memorable number of song sections and repeat them appropriately.

Sounds the Same

Do all your songs sound the same, or, does your song sound similar to an existing popular song? Here are a few tricks for breaking sameness in your songwriting.

1. Try writing your song melody acappella (vocal only, without an instrument or sound track). In this way you are more likely to match your chords accurately to the melody instead of sticking with the chords you are most comfortable using.

2. Once a song is completed, try performing and/or arranging the same song on a different lead instrument. If the song was written on a guitar, for instance, then try it on a piano with a slightly slower tempo. If the song was composed on piano, then try it slightly up-tempo with an electric guitar.

3. For an interesting variation to test your song, try switching the time signature from 4/4 to 6/8. You may not like the end result, but I bet it will get you thinking differently.

4. Do a musical arrangement with "loops" using a digital software program like "GarageBand." By starting with an idea that is outside of your own creative scope, you will often stumble into new melodies and rhythms.

5. Co-writing is another great key to achieving variation.

6. A good idea is to write a song using a different song form than you normally use. If you always write in a Verse-Chorus song form, then try a Chorus-Bridge (also called AABA), or, Verse Only song form (also called AAA.)

Using these variations along with the seven different sources of inspiration presented in this book should deliver you out of sameness.

Does it Deliver?

The final question to ask yourself about the song is "Does it deliver?" There is a rule in songwriting that says, "Don't bore us...get to the chorus."

Sometimes the verses or the song intro are so long that a person loses interest before the song hook arrives.

It is interesting to note that most record producers listen to the first thirty seconds of a song. If they feel like it isn't going anywhere within that time frame, then they will skip to the next song. Producers do this because they know the average listener must be captured in the first thirty seconds.

Long intros, long verses, or a monotonous melody line can cause a person to lose interest before your song hook is delivered. Your verses should be like a mountain climbing expedition—the climb had better be worth the view!

Make sure your song hook is strong and memorable, and that the climb is not too long or difficult to follow. And also make sure your song melody builds and rises to a satisfying conclusion.

Chapter Nine

Finishing a Song

Most of this book has been focused on the subject of inspiring a great song idea, but songs must also be finished.

Finishing a song can actually be more difficult than getting started. I find too great challenges when it comes to the issue of finishing a song.

The first challenge to finishing a song comes from those who release their songs to early. They record their songs or introduce them to a congregation before they have tested the song anywhere.

It reminds me of a relay race I ran in high school. I was the third position runner in a four-man relay team--the guy who passed the baton to the last runner who would finish the race. On this particular hot summer day, I finished my lap, passing off the baton to the fourth runner with a healthy lead. As he came around the final turn, the fans began to cheer in the stands because there was not another runner anywhere in sight. The runner heard the cheering crowd and thought that he had crossed the finish line. He began to dance around and celebrate while other runners passed him by. He celebrated before he had crossed the actual finish line and we lost the race from a commanding lead position.

So often I hear great song ideas hidden in the drab garments of an average song. Inwardly, I wish I could have met with the person before they released their song. An average song rarely has the spiritual or emotional impact that it could have had if it were better crafted. Before releasing a song in any form to the general public it is advisable to get some constructive feedback from others. I encourage writers to find or form a critique group for song revisions. The group can include musicians, pastors or teachers, and congregants who don't consider themselves particularly musical. The musicians speak to the musical aspects of the song; a pastor or teacher can advise on the clarity and accuracy of the lyrical content; a non-musician can judge your singability and hook appeal. Ask your critique group to examine the lyrics for clarity and accuracy. Do any lines seem obscure, biblically inaccurate or unclear?

Next examine the melody. Sing the song for your critique group through one time. Ask them to sing it with you the second time. How hard is it for the average singer to follow the melody? A great melody line can be hummed, whistled, or sung by someone after hearing the song one time. Listen for how they sing the song. Do they take any short cuts? Do they change the melody or drop out at certain places? Consider changing your melody to match what is most natural for the average singer. Are any words or lines particularly hard to sing? Discuss what lyric or melody line might be easier to sing that carries the same meaning. If the praise and worship song is meant to be congregational, always yield your preference to the audience who the song is serving.

Once your song has undergone the revisions of a trusted peer group, you should seek an appropriate window for introducing it to your congregation. This might be a small group, prayer meeting, or congregational gathering. I like to sing a new song during an offering time, altar time, or pre-service when people are not necessarily focused on the song. The goal of presenting the song in one of these forums is to familiarize people with the song without the pressure of trying to follow it. Next, when the song is actually presented in a song service or as an official part of the meeting I again pay attention to how people are responding to the song. Get feedback from your leadership team or critique group on how well they feel the song was received. Remember that every song has a season and worship writers will tend to write ahead of where their congregations are currently at. Be patient. Wait for the right season to introduce a song. Make necessary revision and rewrites. You don't need a hundred more songs sitting in a notebook. You really are looking for one great song that captures the heart of the people and releases them in a fresh expression of worship.

Battling Perfectionism

The second challenge in finishing a song is perfectionism. Most musicians are plagued with some level of perfectionism that can keep them from ever releasing a single song. There are several keys to breaking the perfectionist mindset. The first key for me is remembering that in worship writing I am serving the people not myself. There will always be songs that I sing in the secret place that are just for my personal interaction with God. Ultimately though, a worship writer must be humble and vulnerable enough to share their songs with others and endure the potential critique.

Fear is a robber. Don't let fear stop you from sharing a song with a safe critique group. Not expecting your song to be perfect the first time is another key to breaking perfectionism. If you are writing for the body then you must be willing to let them speak into the song. You don't walk into a restaurant and start ordering for the other patrons. Why should you expect to write for people you won't receive input from? Try not to be overly emotionally attached to how your song currently goes.

Another key to breaking the perfectionist mindset is to discard an "all or nothing" attitude. Someone with this inexperienced mindset receives a little constructive feedback and then throws the whole song in the trash. Rarely will a song be perfect after a first writing. Expect revisions, and welcome input into your song. Those with a teachable, open spirit will be much better equipped to serve the Body with their songwriting.

A feedback group can also encourage you to release your songs. If you can't find or create a song critique forum or if you would rather begin the critique with strangers, then search for song share forums online. There are many online worship forums available where you can post lyrics and MP3-versions of your songs for others to comment on. Some people feel less intimidated submitting their songs in a non-personal forum. Ultimately, if your song receives good reviews on one of these online forums, then you will still need to present it to the leadership of your local church.

Obtaining Copyrights

I'm often asked questions about copyrighting and marketing or producing songs. Before entering any business venture with your original music, it is wise to get good legal counsel and have them review any potential contracts that could be legally binding.

Copyrighting is an easy process and can be done online at the U.S. copyright office. There are also many online services where you can pay to have your songs copyrighted.

However, consider how the copyright law reads at present:

> *"...Under the present copyright law, which became effective January 1, 1978, a work is automatically protected by copyright when it is created. A work is created when it is 'fixed' in a copy or phonorecord for the first time. Neither registration in the Copyright Office nor publication is required for copyright protection under the law."*

The advantage of a copyright registration with the U.S. government is the establishing of a public record of a copyright claim for proof in case of a copyright infringement suit. At the time of this writing, an electronic copyright takes about four and a half months to process online or fifteen months by mail and costs somewhere between $35-$50.

For those living outside the U.S.A., under international law (the Berne Convention), copyright is the automatic right of the creator of the work. This means that copyright exists as soon as you have a tangible version of the music, such as sheet music and/or CDs. This is why many people just mail a copy of their song to themselves and leave the return envelope sealed with the postal date and code on it. I am not advising you to copyright using a certain method, but rather informing you to the possibilities that exist under current copyright law.

In the U.S. you may protect the copyright ownership of

your songs by registering them with the Library of Congress. Information on registering your songs and the necessary forms are available at www.copyright.gov., or you may call 202-707-5959.

Others Using Your Song

Production is a completely different issue. What if someone wants to record or perform your song in a church service? It is usually a good thing if someone wants to record or perform your song.

For recordings, a mechanical royalty based on the "statutory rate" is paid for every recording a person manufactures on a fixed medium, such as CD or downloadable MP3s. The current rate at the time of this writing is 9.1 cents per song, but the royalty rate regularly increases. The copyright and/or publisher of the song are paid for all copies in advance of the recording or every month as they are manufactured or sold.

For church performance of a song I recommend registering the song with the Christian Copyright Licensing International (CCLI) if your song is being sung in five or more churches. This is the minimum usage for CCLI to process your song. Local churches report quarterly usage to CCLI and royalties are paid based on how many churches are currently singing, photocopying, and displaying lyrics for your songs. Visit "Copyright Owners FAQs" at www.ccli.com for more information.

In my thirty years of serving the Christian and secular music industry as a writer, performer, and worship leader, I have had one song and a few song ideas stolen, but this occurs rarely.

In my opinion it always pays to be generous and to

encourage others to use and enjoy your songs. After all, the songs you write are for others to sing.

Don't see yourself as a "one hit wonder." You have a wealth of great songs and song ideas in you. Perform due diligence in protecting your songs, but don't be stingy or over-cautious. One hundred percent of the profits from an unreleased song amounts to nothing; but even a small profit percentage of a released song is something.

Conclusion

Sources of inspiration for great song ideas are everywhere and there are certainly more than the seven I have presented in this book. My goal is to get you unstuck from creative writer's block or from intimidation. The sixth century Chinese philosopher Lao-tzu said:

> *"A journey of a thousand miles begins with a single step."*

If you have never written a song before, then I hope this book has inspired you to start today by composing your first Scripture song. Even if you only get one song section completed or find one great hook, you will have begun an exciting journey.

If you are an experienced writer looking for new ideas, I suggest you read again through the seven sources of inspiration listed in this book. Which of the seven ideas have you already explored? Which sources of inspiration are new to you? Commit yourself to writing songs from each of the seven sources as presented in this book.

As you take on these personal challenges in your songwriting, it will broaden your creative bandwidth and open up new vistas of spiritual perspective.

Perhaps your next step as an experienced worship writer is to form or seek out a critique group and make your song vulnerable to a wider audience. When forming a critique group, it is a good idea to develop a few values for how your group will operate.

Some of the values we hold in our critique group are:

- Honor one another
- Risk and remain teachable
- Truth and honesty wrapped in grace and love

Establishing values creates a safe place for being vulnerable with the createive craft of songwriting, but can still be a place where you receive valuable critique for rewriting or co-writing songs.

My prayer for you is that God would open the eyes of your heart to the song ideas all around you. I pray that your songs would sweep you and others away into realms of transforming God encounters. May you be courageous in sharing your songs with others and wisely skilled in your song craft.

Father, release your new songs in the hearts of your people and may there be great overflowing joy in the journey.

Bibliographic Sources

1   2 Timothy 3:16, Robert Young Literal
    Translation 1862, 1887, 1898 Info

2   Article from www.crosswalk.com

3   Ibid

4   Ephesians 5:19

5   Songs from Heaven, www.Integritymusic.com

6   www.insideworship.com/library/
    Articles/2148/1/The_Heart_And_Skill_Of_
    Writing_Songs_For_Worship_

7   1989 Maranatha Praise, Inc. (Admin. by The
    Copyright Company)

8   Article from www.crosswalk.com

9   Words and Music by Martin Luther, 1592

10 Harper Collins, C. 1961

11 www.insideworship.com/library/
    Articles/2148/1/The_Heart_And_Skill_Of_
    Writing_Songs_For_Worship_

12 www.cyberhymnal.org/htm/i/t/itiswell.htm

13 www.insideworship.com/library/
    Articles/2148/1/The_Heart_And_Skill_Of_
    Writing_Songs_For_Worship_

14 www.ccli.com/WorshipResources/SongStories.
    cfm?itemID=7

15 1 Cor. 13:9

16   Matt. 25:14-28

17   www.insideworship.com/library/Articles/2148/1/
     The_Heart_And_Skill_Of_Writing_Songs_For_
     Worship_

18   Ibid

19   www.taxi.com/transmitter0401/headlineA0401.
     html

20   www.learnathome.com/541240.html

About the Author

Dan McCollam travels internationally as a prophetic speaker and trainer. He strategizes with churches and individuals to create prophetic cultures in which everyone can hear God, activate and mobilize their prophetic words, and express their own unique prophetic diversity.

Dan has developed many resources that offer a fresh perspective on the prophetic, supernatural Kingdom life, biblical character and spiritual gifting. He is well-known as a great friend of the Holy Spirit and one who carries and imparts wisdom, revelation, and breakthrough.

Dan serves on the teaching faculty of Bethel School of the Prophets and the School of Worship in Redding, California. He is part of the Global Legacy apostolic team that oversees a growing number of churches in partnership for revival. He serves on the leadership team at his home church, The Mission, in Vacaville, California, with his wife Regina, and is a director of Deeper School of Supernatural Life also in Vacaville.

Sounds of the Nations and iWar

After serving as a worship leader for 20 years and releasing Kingdom worshipers locally, regionally, and globally on countless mission trips to nations around the world, Dan became heart-sick over the westernization of worship in the majority of churches in which he ministered. Indigenous sounds had often been labeled sinful by church leadership. Since the sounds of every tribe and nation are heard in heaven, becoming an agent in restoring the stolen authentic expressions of worship became a driving passion for Dan, and Sounds of the Nations was born.

As international director of Sounds of the Nations and the Institute for Worship Arts Resources (iWar), Dan trains indigenous peoples to write and record worship songs using their own ethnic sounds, styles, languages, and instruments.

BRIAN&JENN JOHNSON

Brian and Jenn Johnson are the Senior Worship Pastors at Bethel Church, in Redding, California. They also oversee Bethel School of Worship and are involved with Bethel Music. Their mission is to empower people to experience God's Kingdom and His manifest Presence through worship and to equip worship leaders to do the same.

In addition to their own music projects, they are featured on all of the Bethel Live albums, as well as the newly released *The Loft Sessions,* and have written popular songs including "One Thing Remains," "Love Came Down," "God I look to You," and "O Taste and See." Brian and Jenn live in Redding, California with their three wonderful children and spend their free time doing life with friends and family.

For more information about Brian and Jenn Johnson and their music, visit iBethel.org or iTunes.

For more resources
from Dan McCollam,
visit iBethel.com
online store and search for
"Sounds of the Nations"
or "Dan McCollam."
Original worship music from
Sounds of the Nations
is also available on iTunes.

Worship Writer's Songwriting Course

Dan McCollam
A 12-Lesson Course in MP3 Format

Worship Writers Songwriting Course is a 12-part MP3 audio teaching in a live radio show format that equips you to write great praise and worship songs.

Also included are all of the teaching notes and 30 songwriting assignments in PDF format for an interactive songwriting experience.

MP3 Download : $25.00

Worship at the Next Level
Dan McCollam

Discover a fresh breakthrough in your worship experience. Learn the keys of worshipping at:

- The level of your revelation
- The level of your warfare
- The level of your desperation

Break into a whole new place in your God encounter!

Number of CD's : 1   CD Audio: $10   MP3 Download: $4

God's Favorite Word for Praise
Dan McCollam

Many Christians express their praise and worship according to their own comfort level, preference, or religious tradition.

Yet Scripture clearly identifies how God desires to be praised. This CD audio teaching explores the 7 Hebrew words for praise mentioned most often in Scripture. Each brief word study gives you a clearer picture of what it means to be the kind of worshiper God is looking for.

Far from presenting a merely religious argument, this CD imparts a healing anointing and releases a strong affirmation of God's love and joy over you.

Number of CD's : 1 CD-Audio : $10.00 MP3 Download : $4

God Vibrations
Dan McCollam

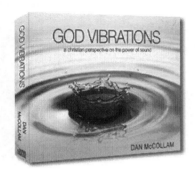

This 4-CD audio series presents a Christian perspective on the power of sound.

Genesis 1:3 says, "The Spirit of God moved upon the face of the deep." Those God vibrations were the beginning of all created things.

CD 1 - Sound Foundations   **CD 2** - Destructive Power
CD 3 - Creative Power   **CD 4** - Sound's Healing Influence
Number of CD's : 4   **DVD** Available $35

Living on the Right Side of the Cross
Dan McCollam

What really happened on the cross? What did Jesus mean when he shouted, "It is finished?" Are you living merely forgiven or totally free?

Dan McCollam believes the cross frees us from a primary struggle with ourselves, releasing us into a pursuit of our own destiny and the destruction of the kingdom of darkness.

Originally delivered at Graham Cooke's Permission Granted conference.

Number of CD's : 1   CD Audio: $10   MP3 Download: $4

Limitless: Living the Ascended Life
Dan McCollam

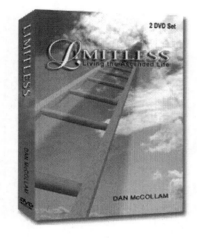

Recorded at Graham Cooke's "Limitless Possibilities" Conference in Vacaville, California, this two-part series explores the believer's limitless inheritance in Jesus Christ.

Disc One: Enter the Land of the Limitless through an understanding of the true glory of the cross. Discover how the cross of Jesus Christ is meant for more than forgiveness but also freedom from sin and fullness of all that fills God Himself.

Disc Two: Living in the Land of the Limitless explores the key to breakthrough. Discover how to follow-through on revelations, supernatural experiences, and God encounters to expand their impact on your daily life. This teaching is loaded with practical principles and applications.

Available Options:

Number of DVD's : 2 **$35.00**   Number of CD's : 2 **$15.00**

MP3 Download : **$8.00**

Made in the USA
San Bernardino, CA
15 July 2017